SCENT IN THE GARDEN

Create a fragrant paradise to enjoy throughout the
year, shown in over 100 stunning photographs

ANDREW MIKOLAJSKI

LORENZ BOOKS

This edition is published by Lorenz Books
an imprint of Anness Publishing Ltd
Blaby Road, Wigston, Leicestershire LE18 4SE
info@anness.com

www.lorenzbooks.com; www.annesspublishing.com

If you like the images in this book and would like to investigate using
them for publishing, promotions or advertising, please visit our website
www.practicalpictures.com for more information.

A CIP catalogue record for this book
is available from the British Library.

Publisher: Joanna Lorenz
Editor: Valerie Ferguson
Photography: Peter Anderson, Jonathan Buckley, John Freeman,
Michelle Garrett, Andrea Jones, Marie O'Hara and Polly Wreford;
p56: Diana Yakely (garden designer)
Series Designer: Larraine Shamwana
Designer: Andrew Heath
Production Manager: Steve Lang

PUBLISHER'S NOTE

Although the advice and information in this book are believed to be accurate and
true at the time of going to press, neither the authors nor the publisher can
accept any legal responsibility or liability for any errors or omissions that may
have been made nor for any inaccuracies nor for any loss, harm or injury that
comes about from following instructions or advice in this book.

CONTENTS

Introduction

SCENT IS OFTEN THE MOST MEMORABLE ELEMENT OF A GARDEN, EVEN MORE POTENT IN ITS IMPACT THAN FLOWER COLOUR OR THE HARMONY OF SHAPES AND TEXTURES. THE FAINTEST WHIFF OF FRAGRANCE CAN UNLOCK THE DOOR TO A HOST OF MEMORIES.

In the plant kingdom scent functions only to attract pollinators, but for the gardener it is the most elusive of all the senses and the hardest to define. Scents cannot be recorded and transmitted like sounds or images, nor is it always easy to put into words how we experience them. Moreover, our sense of smell is notoriously under-developed compared with that of the cats, dogs and other domestic animals we share our lives with.

There is even a variation of sensitivity within the human species itself. Some people seem to have a highly developed sense of smell while others have the misfortune to lose the faculty altogether. While women are said to have the keener sense of smell, according to Dr Alex Comfort, men are more responsive to it, so there is no battle of the sexes here.

Our reactions to scent tend to be individual, and it is not always easy to pinpoint a particular aroma. Although we might be able to distinguish between two or three different scents, if more are added the nose becomes anaesthetized, making distinctions difficult. Scent can, however, be used to produce

Above: *The evening primrose* (Oenothera biennis) *releases its fragrance at night.*

Above: Hypericum *'Hidcote' is a useful plant for ground cover and has leaves that are aromatic when crushed.*

seem to belong to a further group, with citrus or lemon overtones. These fragrances are almost universally perceived as pleasant and exhilarating.

Citrus smells are light and refreshing, while herbal ones, such as thyme and lavender, tend to have a calming effect. Some herbal scents are more astringent, however, with notes of eucalyptus that not everyone finds pleasing, although many experience them as invigorating.

A musk-like odour can often be detected in honey-scented plants, and such fragrances seem warm and enduring. They are most commonly encountered among the orchids.

Some flower scents combine more than one note and seem to be "layered". We usually think of these as exotic, as they can be so rich and heady as to be almost cloying.

a sense of calm and wellbeing, or, conversely, to stimulate and invigorate, ensuring that your garden is a place of regeneration as well as tranquillity.

TYPES OF SCENT

Difficult to describe though they are, scents in the garden can be divided into several broad groups.

The commonest examples are usually defined as aromatic. They are generally sweetly spicy and always appealing: we seem never to tire of them. They are found in the almond-like fragrance of heliotropes and the clove essence of carnations and pinks. Violet scents are sharper and more transitory. As well as violets (*Viola*), mignonettes (*Reseda*) and *Iris reticulata* belong to this group.

Roses are usually fruity and spicy, pleasing both up close and at a distance. Some tulips also have this type of scent. Interestingly, many roses

Above: Perovskia *smells of eucalyptus.*

5

Introduction

*Above: Creeping thymes (*Thymus*) can be planted to be trodden gently underfoot.*

BENEFITS OF SCENTED PLANTS

Apart from the pleasure they give to gardeners, scented plants are of inestimable value to the garden's ecology, given their appeal to pollinating insects. A diverse insect population is the best way of keeping down garden pests – whose attacks on plants also make them vulnerable to disease – since their predators are more likely to be present.

Brightly coloured plants are usually designed to attract birds, which have no sense of smell, so such flowers are often scentless. Many of the most fragrant plants have simple, cup-shaped flowers, for easy access to the pollen.

Night-scented plants have evolved to attract moths and other nocturnal insects. These plants include night-scented stock (*Matthiola longipetala* subsp. *bicornis*), tobacco plants (*Nicotiana*) and the exquisitely fragrant South American sub-shrub, willow-leaved jessamine (*Cestrum parqui*).

HOW TO RECOGNIZE SCENTED PLANTS

Latin botanical names often provide good clues as to whether a plant is scented or not. Any genus name followed by the descriptive word *fragrantissima*, *odora* or *suaveolens* is bound to be fragrant. Sometimes the type of scent is indicated: *citriodora* means lemon-scented, and *moschata* means musky. But beware: *pungens* implies a strong (or pungent) scent that is not necessarily appealing.

Scent is not always betrayed by the name, however: *Magnolia grandiflora* refers only to the size of the flowers, not to their bewitching fragrance.

Above: The characteristic scent of Eucalyptus *is carried by its volatile oils.*

6

Parts of the Plant

Speak of scent in the garden and most people immediately think of flowers. While it is true that in most cases it is the flowers that provide the most intoxicating of garden fragrances, other parts of plants can be aromatic, even though they must sometimes be crushed, rubbed or bruised to release their attraction. This is the case with most herbs, but there are other well-known garden plants that have "secret" scents. *Hypericum* 'Hidcote' is widely grown for its yellow flowers and robust qualities, but its aromatic leaves give it a distinction of quite a different kind. *Perovskia*, a sub-shrub valued for its hardiness and late summer lavender-coloured flowers, has white-bloomed stems that smell of eucalyptus oil. Such scents are not always appealing, however: the crushed leaves of skimmias have a somewhat bitter note.

Anyone who has wandered through an apple orchard in autumn will recall the evocative, slightly alcoholic cider smell that arises from bruised windfalls. On a warm day you will see wasps buzzing drunkenly around, intoxicated by the fermenting juices.

Gum trees (*Eucalyptus*) have resinous bark, as do most conifers, so the many genera are not listed separately here. *Chimonanthus* has fragrant leaves, wood, flowers and seeds and is a delight in the winter garden.

Above: *'Constance Spry', one of the most richly scented of all roses, is superb when trained against a wall.*

PLANTS WITH AROMATIC WOOD, BARK OR LEAVES

Aloysia triphylla
Cercidiphyllum (fallen leaves)
Cistus
Eucalyptus
Helichrysum italicum
Hypericum 'Hidcote'
Laurus nobilis
Liquidambar styraciflua
Myrtus communis
Perovskia
Populus balsamifera
Rosmarinus officinalis
Ruta graveolens
Santolina
Skimmia
Thymus

COMBINING PLANTS

Devising a planting scheme that includes a large proportion of strongly scented plants can be even more difficult than planning a colour scheme, for which you can at least get some ideas by playing around with colour swatches. Trying to balance and harmonize the whole range of natural aromas and notes in a collection of plants is a more abstract process, since you cannot reproduce garden scents in the comfort of your sitting room.

On the whole, within a single bed scents are best in pairs or at a maximum of three. More confuse the nose and can seem to anaesthetize it, meaning that none of the scents makes its full impact. Rich, heavy smells are best combined with lighter, fresher

Above: *Bergamot (*Monarda*) is an aromatic that can be used in potpourri.*

Above: *Conifers such as* Thuja plicata, *with resinous bark, are highly scented.*

scents: hence the value of underplanting roses with lavender. Alternatives would be old-fashioned, clove-infused carnations (*Dianthus*) – especially if you have alkaline soil – or sweet violets (*Viola*). Some scents are best appreciated on their own, and that applies especially to the powerfully scented *Magnolia grandiflora*, with its lemon-scented, waxy-textured flowers. It is often best to combine such plants with non-scented ones. For example, you could introduce a sweetly scented mock orange (*Philadelphus*) into a white garden if you are relying on 'Iceberg' as the main rose, since this has only a light fragrance. For scent later in the year add some lilies, such as *Lilium regale*, or plant the creamy white *Paeonia* 'White Wings'.

SITING PLANTS

Finding the right position in the garden for your scented plants can increase their impact considerably.

Where you site the plants will largely depend on how they distribute their scent. The mock orange, for example, a large shrub that wafts its scent far and wide, is ideal for the back of a large border, especially since it is rather dull when out of flower. But large plants whose flowers you want to bury your head in, such as *Rosa* 'Constance Spry', need to be sited for easy access, and they are ideally trained over a pergola spanning a walkway or against a house wall, close to where you sit in the evening. House walls are also ideal for other scented climbers, such as the vigorous jasmine (*Jasminum polyanthum*) and the deliciously fragrant star jasmine (*Trachelospermum jasminoides*).

A sheltered garden will seem to trap scent, making a veritable bower of fragrance. In a more open, windy site, locate the most sheltered areas (such as in the lee of a wall or a group of shrubs) and place your fragrant plants there, otherwise you will scarcely notice the scent because it will be borne away on the breeze.

Plants that need to be touched to release their fragrance, such as the herbs lavender (*Lavandula*) and rosemary (*Rosmarinus*), should be placed where you can rub their leaves as you pass. Some prostrate plants are tough enough to stand the occasional (light) footfall and can be planted in

Above: The leaves of Skimmia japonica *have a curious, rather bitter aroma that is released when they are crushed.*

Above: Pelargonium triste *is an unusual member of this genus: its flowers emit a freesia-like scent at night.*

Seasonal Factors

Aromatic plants, such as the conifers and woody herbs that originated in Mediterranean countries, give off most scent during hot weather, so you will be particularly aware of them in high summer. Other plants, however, seem to smell sweeter during mild, damp weather or after a shower of rain, when the moisture in the atmosphere holds the scent in some way. You will particularly notice the scent of the late-flowering climbing rose 'New Dawn' on a cool, damp morning in early autumn. Winter-flowering plants tend to be at their most fragrant on mild, sunny days, when their pollinators stir from their dormancy.

the cracks in paving to make a scented carpet. The creeping thymes (*Thymus*) are ideal for this purpose, but you could try the slightly less robust camomile (*Chamaemelum nobile*), *Rosmarinus prostratus* or pennyroyal (*Mentha pulegium*), which are also ideal plants for the top of a retaining wall or the edge of a raised bed.

Many scented plants can be grown in containers and placed on a patio where you sit out in summer. Some are suitable for window boxes or hanging baskets that can be suspended from a pergola over a patio or near a barbecue area. A position near an open window will allow you to enjoy the fragrance from indoors.

Above: Like most members of the pea family, laburnums produce sweetly scented flowers.

NIGHT AND DAY

Unlike other attributes, such as colour, texture and shape, scent is not a constant. Flowers give off their scent when their pollinators are active. Often this is during the hottest part of the day, and there are few more evocative sights and sounds than those of bees, moving from flower to flower on a hot summer day, collecting pollen. Those that are most fragrant when dew is in the air will smell most strongly early in the day and at dusk.

NIGHT-SCENTED PLANTS
Brugmansia suaveolens
Cestrum parqui
Hemerocallis citrina
Matthiola longipetala subsp. bicornis
Mirabilis jalapa
Nicotiana alata
Oenothera biennis
Pelargonium triste
Reseda odorata

Above: The epiphytic orchid Oncidium *'Sharry Baby' has striking flowers that smell of chocolate.*

A few precious plants are scented at night because they are pollinated by night-flying insects. They are particularly appreciated by those who have daytime jobs and who look forward to the delights of a fragrant evening garden at the end of a stressful day.

HOW TO USE THIS BOOK

This quick and easy guide to planning a scented garden begins with a section, *Getting Started*, containing practical advice. *Scented Plants in the Garden* describes the main plant groups, and *Scent for All Seasons* explains how those plants can be used to give all-year-round fragrance. Finally, *Scent for Every Style* suggests ways in which gardens can be designed to include many favourite aromas.

11

Getting Started

IF YOUR PLANTS ARE TO DO WELL, THEY NEED TO BE GROWN IN THE
CONDITIONS THAT SUIT THEM. NOT GIVING PLANTS WHAT THEY WANT
CAN BRING DISAPPOINTING RESULTS, BUT FOLLOWING THE GUIDELINES
HERE SHOULD ENSURE IMPROVED GARDEN PERFORMANCE.

SOIL CONDITIONS

Some plants are indifferent to soil
type and will tolerate a range of
conditions, but many are more
demanding. Taking a little care at the
planning stage pays dividends. Not
only will the plants perform to their
best, but they will be strong-growing,
healthy and disease-resistant.

Acid or Alkaline?

Some plants are sensitive to the degree
of acidity/alkalinity in the soil. This is
expressed in terms of the pH scale, on
which 7 indicates neutral. A pH below
7 is acid and above, up to 14, is alkaline. Most soils have a pH of around
6–6.5 and are, therefore, slightly acid.

The best way to find out whether
your soil is acid or alkaline is by
means of a chemical test, for which
kits are available at garden centres.
These are cheap and simple to use and
give results that are accurate enough
for most garden purposes. It is also a
good idea to look at what is growing
well in neighbouring gardens or in the
surrounding countryside. The presence
of rhododendrons, camellias and
heathers would suggest that the soil is

*Above: Use a soil testing kit to ascertain
whether your soil is acid or alkaline
before choosing plants for your garden.*

acid. Elders, clematis, *Dianthus* and
birches indicate alkaline conditions.
But beware: pockets of acid soil can
occur in predominantly alkaline areas
and vice versa. It is even possible to
find variations within a single garden,
so if you do a chemical test, it is advis-
able to test the soil in different areas.

Light or Heavy?

Possibly even more important than
soil pH is the texture of the soil, which
determines how much moisture it is
capable of holding and hence just how
fertile it is likely to be. Take a handful

Above: Spent mushroom compost (soil mix) is a good organic material to use as a soil improver, but it tends to be alkaline.

Above: Add grit to soil if it is at all heavy or sticky, to open up the texture and improve drainage.

of soil and squeeze it together. If it binds into loose crumbs, which you can rub through your fingers like pastry, you have the ideal texture – a friable loam. If it fails to adhere and runs through your fingers like dust, you have a light, dry, sandy soil. If it binds like modelling clay, holding the marks of your fingers, it is heavy clay.

Light soils are easy to work and quick to warm up, but they are low in nutrients. They favour the Mediterranean plants that need good drainage. Heavy soils are cold but usually fertile, since they hold moisture well. They suit robust, tap-rooted plants and others that demand a lot of nutrients. Most plants will thrive in a moist but well-drained loam.

Soil Improvement

All soils are improved by the addition of organic matter, dug into the soil before planting or spread around the plants as a mulch in spring or autumn.

Best of all is home-made garden compost, made from soft plant material (including vegetable trimmings from the kitchen) that has been piled up and allowed to rot down over six months to a year. Spent hops and mushroom compost are alternatives. Well-rotted farmyard manure is excellent for bulking up light soils. Proprietary brands of soil improver are also available bagged up at garden centres.

Above: Lily-of-the-valley (Convallaria majalis) likes moist, rich soil.

13

The Right Aspect

Most plants have a preference for either sun or shade, although some will tolerate either position. Few plants, however, will flower happily in deep shade, lily-of-the-valley being an exception. Bear this in mind when planning your planting if you are choosing species for the sake of their scented flowers.

Mediterranean plants thrive in full sun, which brings out the fragrance of their essential oils. They can also cope with windy conditions as many of them grow wild on hillsides.

Judicious Pruning

Most woody plants – shrubs, climbers and herbs – need pruning from time to time to keep them in shape, maintain their vigour and encourage the production of flowering wood, which is essential if they are to keep bearing

Above: *Clip over heathers with shears or secateurs (pruners).*

Above: *The fragrant rose 'Margaret Merril' lasts wonderfully well as a cut flower.*

the fragrant flowers for which they are grown. Most spring-flowering shrubs should be pruned immediately after flowering, which gives them ample time to develop new wood for next year. Late flowerers, such as roses and some buddlejas, which flower on new wood, should be pruned in early spring, before they start into growth. You can prune most deciduous plants in midwinter when they are dormant.

Cut out any dead, diseased or damaged wood. Also cut out any older, unproductive wood, to the base of the plant if necessary. Shorten the remainder of the stems by one-third to half their length to create a balanced, open plant. You will probably be able to leave some stems unpruned.

Heathers can be trimmed lightly after flowering with shears, and lavenders should be clipped to shape before flowering, in spring.

FLOWERS FOR CUTTING

It is natural to want to enjoy some of the fragrance of the garden in your home, but not all flowers are suitable for cutting, either because the flowers are not borne on long stems or because they are short-lived in water.

Cut flowers for the house early in the morning or in the evening, and choose flowers that are about to open: fully open blooms will not last as long.

POTPOURRI

Some scented plants can be dried for enjoyment out of season. For this purpose, the plants need to be as dry as possible, so cut them on a fine day in summer. Hang them in loose bunches in a dry, airy place. If you can exclude light, so much the better, since they

---

SCENTED PLANTS FOR CUTTING
Amberboa moschata
Convallaria majalis
Dianthus
Erysimum
Iris
Lathyrus odoratus
Lilium
Monarda
Narcissus
Rosa

---

will retain their colour longer. If you prefer, dry the stems on silica gel, available from florists and craft shops.

When the stems are dry, either strip the leaves and flowers from them for mixing in shallow bowls as potpourri or use the stems whole to scent a linen closet or drawer.

AROMATIC PLANTS FOR POTPOURRI
Acorus calamus 'Variegatus'
Agastache foeniculum
Aloysia triphylla
Angelica archangelica
Artemisia
Foeniculum vulgare
Geranium macrorrhizum
Houttuynia cordata
Hyssopus
Lavandula
Melissa
Mentha
Monarda
Origanum vulgare
Salvia officinalis
Santolina
Thymus

Above: *All parts of* Angelica archangelica *can be used in potpourri.*

15

Scented Plants in the Garden

EVERY GROUP OF GARDEN PLANTS INCLUDES DELICIOUSLY SCENTED SPECIES, FROM QUICK-TO-GROW ANNUALS TO EXOTIC FLOWERING TREES. THE FOLLOWING SELECTION INCLUDES IDEAS TO HELP YOU FILL A GARDEN WITH FRAGRANCE, WHATEVER ITS SIZE AND STYLE.

BULBS AND CORMS

Valued primarily for their vivid bursts of colour, many of the flowers that grow from bulbs and corms also supply a rich fragrance that more than doubles their appeal. Try to mass them, where possible, to make the most of their brief but intoxicating moments of glory.

Bulbs and corms are among the most versatile plants in the garden, and most are easy to grow. Early bulbs, usually dwarf, are harbingers of spring, studding the bare earth with jewel-like colours, often at the coldest time of the year. Bulbs are also excellent in containers, and this is much

Above: Muscari armeniacum *is a diminutive plant with a delicate scent – good for planting* en masse *in the garden.*

the best way to appreciate the scent of low-growing species that you cannot get down low enough to sniff in the garden. Crocuses, dwarf narcissi, irises, tulips and grape hyacinths can all be grown in shallow pans of gritty compost (soil mix).

Some early bulbs are traditionally grown for enjoyment indoors, notably hyacinths (*Hyacinthus*) and *Narcissus papyraceus*. Remember that these are by no means hot-house plants. They are adapted to a hard life, so keep them outdoors in a cool, light but sheltered spot (perhaps against a house wall) and bring them indoors only when the flower buds start to show colour. After flowering they can be planted outside.

Freesias and *Hymenocallis*, which are not hardy in cold climates, can be grown in pots in an alpine house. Florists' cyclamen (usually unnamed varieties of *Cyclamen persicum*) are sold as winter-flowering houseplants. As they are always sold in flower you can be sure to choose the most fragrant. They enjoy a cool but light position. Store them dry in summer and water and feed in autumn to bring them back into growth.

Summer bulbs include the glorious lilies, though many garden forms are not scented. Look for the species *Lilium regale* and the later-flowering *L. speciosum*. The sumptuously fragrant

BULBS WITH FRAGRANT FLOWERS
Amaryllis belladonna
Crinum
Crocus
Cyclamen persicum
Freesia
Galanthus
Galtonia candicans
Gladiolus tristis
Hyacinthus
Hymenocallis
Iris reticulata
Lilium (some)
Muscari
Narcissus
Tulipa clusiana
Tulipa sylvestris

Easter lily (*L. longiflorum*) is unfortunately not hardy, so must be grown under glass in cold districts. It is easily raised from seed. The bulb season ends with the dramatic South Africans: *Amaryllis belladonna* and *Crinum*, both with trumpet-like flowers.

Above: Lilium regale *is a strongly scented species lily for the summer border.*

Above: *Hyacinths have possibly the most distinctive scent of any bulbous plant.*

17

ANNUALS AND BIENNIALS

An annual is a plant that completes its life cycle within one growing season: the seed germinates, grows, flowers, sets seed and dies all within the space of a year. The seed is dormant until the return of conditions favourable to germination, often the next spring. In the case of biennials, the seed usually germinates as soon as it is set, in summer or autumn, and the young plantlet overwinters to flower the following year (but the process is still completed within twelve months).

Annuals are generally used in the garden for instant impact, for the brilliance of the flowers and the ready way in which they are produced. Quite a few, however, have the advantage of scent, so it is always well worth including some of these. Seeds are usually marketed as strains or mixtures, because the flower colour cannot be guaranteed. New cultivars are introduced regularly, so consult the latest catalogues to keep abreast of these. Some seed merchants produce bundles of scented annuals, and this is a convenient way of creating an instant scented garden.

In addition to a description of the flowers, seed packets carry full instructions on germination and aftercare. If you do not have time to raise plants from seed, buy young plants from a garden centre in spring. However, you will have less choice.

Annuals are almost without exception flowers of high summer, needing warmth and light to perform at their best. Biennials, however, usually flower earlier, in late spring. It is also possible to make a late summer sowing of hardy annuals for overwintering. These will be the earliest to flower in the following season.

Above: *Annual nasturtiums have a light, peppery scent, and both the flowers and young leaves are edible.*

Above: *Sweet peas (*Lathyrus odoratus*), best sown in autumn, are an essential component of any scented garden.*

18

Choosing Varieties for Scent

As a rule, scented annuals are less showy than those grown for splendid flowers, so it is a good idea to mix scented varieties with other strains. Night-scented stock (*Matthiola longipetala* subsp. *bicornis*) is a case in point: it is a spindly plant with modest little flowers of a bleached mauve. Scatter the seed among other plants, such as the showier gillyflower (*M. incana*), for the best of both worlds. Sweet peas (*Lathyrus odoratus*) are typical cottage garden plants. Despite the common name, not all cultivars are equally fragrant, so it is worth experimenting to find a variety that particularly pleases you, and many of the old-fashioned plants are among the most fragrant, if not the most

Above: Sweet-scented Heliotropium *'Marine' is actually a perennial, but it is usually treated as an annual in cold districts.*

colourful. Nasturtiums (*Tropaeolum*) have a fresh, peppery scent, reminiscent of the related watercress. Both flowers and leaves are edible, even if the taste is an acquired one.

ANNUALS AND BIENNIALS WITH SCENTED FLOWERS

Amberboa moschata
Erysimum cheiri
Exacum affine
Iberis
Lathyrus odoratus
Limnanthes douglasii
Lobularia maritima
Matthiola
Oenothera biennis
Reseda odorata
Tropaeolum

SHRUBS AND PERENNIALS

These plants are the mainstay of the garden, flowering year after year and gradually increasing in size and importance. Nowadays, they are frequently used together to make low-maintenance mixed borders that provide interest over a long period.

Aromatic Shrubs

Leaving aside the shrubby herbs, there are a number of shrubs with aromatic foliage, and those that are also evergreen will supply scent all year round.

Many conifers are dwarf and compact or so slow-growing that they can be treated as shrubs for a good few years. They are traditionally combined with heathers, but also work surprisingly well with grasses planted in island beds. But if conifers

Above: Dianthus *'Cobham Beauty' has a light, pleasing scent. Small fragrant pinks make ideal edging plants near a path.*

are not to your taste, try skimmias or Mexican orange blossom (*Choisya ternata*), although you will have to bruise the leaves to enjoy their aroma. The young leaves of the sweet briar (*Rosa eglanteria*) smell distinctly of apples after a shower of rain.

Above: Buddleja alternifolia *has honey-scented flowers in midsummer.*

*Above: The common myrtle (*Myrtus communis*) has an unmistakable aroma.*

Flowering Shrubs

As far as scent is concerned, there is almost a surfeit of shrubs. Mahonias have yellow flowers with a fragrance like lilies-of-the-valley, and some of the berberises, both deciduous and evergreen forms, are similar. *Viburnum* is also a genus richly endowed with flowering species. One of the best is the hybrid *V. × burkwoodii*, an elegant plant with heads of sweetly fragrant white flowers in spring.

The scent of lilacs (*Syringa*) seems to embody late spring, but some of the species have flowers with a fetid smell. The hybrids of *S. vulgaris* have the typical lilac scent.

Buddlejas are indispensable for their honey-scented, mauve, white or purple flowers. The butterfly bush, *Buddleja davidii*, is almost too well known in some gardens, where it self-seeds with abandon. *B. alternifolia* has a more elegant form, particularly when it is trained as a standard.

SCENTED SHRUBS
Berberis sargentiana
Buddleja
Camellia sasanqua
Cestrum parqui
Choisya ternata
Citrus
Cytisus battandieri
Daphne
Deutzia
Elaeagnus × ebbingei
Erica arborea
Hamamelis mollis
Mahonia × media
Myrtus communis
Osmanthus decorus
Philadelphus
Skimmia japonica
Syringa vulgaris
Viburnum

Above: *The late summer-flowering* Buddleja davidii *'Black Knight' is dramatically coloured and richly scented.*

21

Fragrant Roses

If ever a group of plants was prized for its scent, it is the roses. Not all roses are scented, but it is a myth that only old varieties have fragrance. Some, such as 'Nevada', have a light scent, which seems to hang on the air some distance from the plant. Others bear their scent on their stamens, and this is usually a rich, heady fragrance that you have to drink in by burying your nose in the flower.

Scented Perennials

This large and diverse group of plants contains some of the most exquisitely scented species.

The herbaceous clematis are less well known than the climbers, but they make excellent additions to the border, flowering in early summer. *Clematis recta* needs staking but pro-

Above: Besides its unique colouring, Rosa *'Escapade' has a delicious fragrance.*

duces a mass of starry, creamy-white flowers, held on stems up to 1.2m (4ft) tall. Herbaceous peonies also need staking, but few gardeners would

SCENTED ROSES

'Apricot Nectar'
'Blue Moon'
'Buff Beauty'
'Céleste'
'Constance Spry'
'Escapade'
'Fantin-Latour'
'Fragrant Cloud'
'Lady Hillingdon'
'Margaret Merril'
'Mme Hardy'
'Mme Isaac Pereire'
'Reine Victoria'
R. rugosa
'Sheila's Perfume'
'Whisky Mac'

Above: Cytisus battandieri *deserves its common name of pineapple broom. The flowers both look and smell like pineapples.*

think that a problem when confronted by their sumptuous flowers, many blessed with a rich, spicy fragrance unmatched in this group of plants. The pink 'Sarah Bernhardt' is an old but reliable cultivar, and 'Kelway's Supreme' has huge, bowl-shaped, satin-textured flowers, but all the cultivars are ravishing, and specialist nursery catalogues are usually temptingly illustrated. The single-flowered forms are more likely to be scented than those with double flowers.

The daylilies (*Hemerocallis*) now form a huge group. New cultivars have a longer flowering season, and some are night-flowering. Many are sweetly scented, but check the catalogues of the specialist breeders. Lily-of-the-valley (*Convallaria majalis*) is almost too familiar, but it has an unmistakable scent and is ideal for growing in a shady spot. It can be forced for winter flowering indoors if you pot up the "pips" in autumn and bring them into an unheated greenhouse or conservatory (sunroom). A little more warmth in midwinter will produce earlier flowers than appear outside. Give the plants a rest after flowering and return them to a position outdoors.

Carnations and pinks (*Dianthus*) make ideal edging plants, which are attractive when out of flower with their sheaves of steel-blue leaves. The clove-scented cultivars are particularly

SCENTED PERENNIALS
Clematis recta
Convallaria majalis
Cosmos atrosanguineus
Dianthus
Helleborus lividus
Hemerocallis
Hosta plantaginea
Iris unguicularis
Phlox
Primula
Smilacina racemosa
Verbena bonariensis

sought-after. Not all the newer forms are scented, although they have the advantage of a longer season.

One of the most intriguing of all plants is *Cosmos atrosanguineus*, whose blood-red flowers smell of melted chocolate. If you are a chocoholic, this is the plant for you.

Above: *The delicate scent of primula flowers is best appreciated when they are grown in sizeable drifts in a mixed border.*

TREES WITH SCENT

A tree adds dignity and style to a garden, and several species are scented. Choose carefully, however, because not only will a tree often outlive the gardener, but many trees will also eventually outgrow their allotted space.

Flowering Trees

A scented tree in full flower will be one of the glories of the garden. In a mild climate, where frosts are unlikely, an airy acacia, such as *Acacia dealbata* or *A. baileyana*, will charm with its bobbly, duckling-yellow mimosa flowers in early spring. In a cold area, grow it against a warm wall or in a conservatory (sunroom). Acacias are among the few trees that positively thrive in a

TREES WITH SCENTED FLOWERS
Acacia dealbata
Aesculus hippocastanum
Laburnum × *watereri* 'Vossii'
Magnolia delavayi
Magnolia kobus
Magnolia × *loebneri*
Malus floribunda
Malus hupehensis
Prunus 'Amonagawa'
Prunus × *yedoensis*
Styrax japonica
Tilia × *euchlora*
Tilia petiolaris

container. Hardier and rather grander are the magnolias, with sumptuous, chalice-like flowers, usually of a creamy ivory white, although pinks and purples also occur. In cold areas choose a position out of the morning sun, since the flowers can be blackened by a

Above: *The pure white flowers of* Magnolia × loebneri *'Merrill' are delicately scented.*

Above: Acacia dealbata *produces masses of flowers from late winter to early spring – it makes a magnificent specimen in a sheltered garden.*

sudden rise in temperature after a clear, frosty night. Ornamental cherries (*Prunus*), usually prized for the wealth of their blossom, also include some scented cultivars among their number. The same is true of the crab apples (*Malus*). The musty scent of hawthorn blossoms (*Crataegus*), so evocative in the wild, is possibly best kept out of small gardens and its use restricted to boundary planting.

The evergreen Chinese privet would be an unusual choice. Normally used for hedging (in which case the flowers are generally sacrificed by the tight clipping necessary for a neat surface), this makes a surprisingly elegant specimen or back-of-the-border plant. A warning note must be struck, however: not everyone finds the scent of the creamy summer flowers appealing.

Limes (*Tilia*) are too large for most gardens, but anyone who has one growing nearby (such as in a village square or as a pavement planting) will know the heady scent the flowers, though inconspicuous, release on warm evenings in early summer.

Bark, Stems and Leaves

Most conifers are scented, usually because of their sticky, resinous stems. You will especially notice this in a hot summer, when pines (*Pinus*) in particular give off a characteristic scent, but you will also be aware of it if you cut stems from your conifers for winter decoration indoors – do not be put off by the synthetic 'pine fragrance' used in household cleaning products. Eucalyptus scent is also familiar from cough medicines and other remedies.

The scent of the balsam poplar (*Populus balsamifera*) is unmistakable when the leaves unfurl in spring. At the other end of the growing season, one of the most appealing of all scented trees is *Cercidiphyllum*, whose leaves smell of burnt toffee when they fall to the ground in autumn.

> **TREES WITH AROMATIC BARK, WOOD OR LEAVES**
>
> *Cercidiphyllum*
> *Eucalyptus*
> *Laurus nobilis*
> *Liquidambar styraciflua*
> *Populus balsamifera*
> *Populus* × *candicans*

AROMATIC HERBS

Most herbs are not so much scented as aromatic, a quality that is often not immediately apparent but is released only when the leaves or stems are bruised or crushed. The many forms of mint (*Mentha*) are a good example. Most of the plants that are defined as herbs have scents that are refreshing and invigorating, but they are not always appealing. Sometimes a plant's aromatic qualities are a defence mechanism to deter browsing animals. In addition, herbs have been so widely used in medicines that they have acquired connotations beyond gardening. Nevertheless, in any scented garden, herbs will play a major role.

Most of the fragrant herbs have culinary uses, so they are doubly valuable in the garden. Fragrant sage

HERBS WITH SCENTED LEAVES
Aloysia triphylla
Artemisia arborescens
Laurus nobilis
Lavandula
Mentha
Monarda didyma
Ocimum basilicum
Origanum vulgare
Rosmarinus officinalis
Salvia officinalis
Santolina
Thymus

(*Salvia*), rosemary (*Rosmarinus officinalis*) and thyme (*Thymus*) are as well known to cooks as they are to gardeners, but a scented garden will also have room for an aromatic evergreen bay (*Laurus nobilis*) and annual basil (*Ocimum basilicum*). Ornamental herbs, such as the attractive, ever-popular lavender (*Lavandula*) is also grown for its deliciously scented flowers, and cotton lavender (*Santolina chamaecyparissus*) for its aromatic foliage.

Because most of the culinary herbs are native to countries around the Mediterranean, they need to be grown in well-drained soil in full sun. They are particularly well suited to growing in containers, which tend to be well drained and, if space in the garden is limited, can be moved to sunny positions as the plants come into flower. Bear in mind, however, that many of the cultivated forms with golden or variegated foliage will do better in light or dappled shade.

Above: Lemon balm (Melissa officinalis) is very easy to grow and smells strongly of citrus when crushed.

Take care when handling some of these plants, especially common rue (*Ruta graveolens*). People with sensitive skin may be allergic to the foliage, which can cause rashes.

Above: All forms of lavender have that characteristic scent, but the Mediterranean Lavandula stoechas stands out.

Harvesting and Preserving

Many herbs can be used fresh in cooked dishes, added to salads or used to make refreshing tisanes. Such herbs should be grown close to the house to make harvesting easy. Many herbs can also be dried or frozen for use out of season, and drying can sometimes enhance the flavour.

Harvest in fine, sunny weather, picking the leaves and shoots early in the day, when the plants are at their freshest. If you intend to dry the plants, wait until the dew has evaporated before picking. Dry the leaves and stems on a metal rack in a warm, dry, well-ventilated place or in a very low oven. If necessary, the leaves can then be removed from the stems by rubbing. Once dried, herbs should be stored in airtight containers.

*Above: 'Tricolor' is an ornamental variegated form of the culinary herb sage (*Salvia officinalis*).*

CLIMBING PLANTS

Most climbers are naturally big, rampant plants, and this is really part of their charm, since they will cast their scent far and wide.

Trained over pergolas, they can be used to create a delightful shaded place to sit and relax on a warm summer's day, or they can be planted to ramble through trees, which is logical when you consider that this is how they grow in the wild. They can also be grown over shrubs in the border to lengthen the period of interest, flowering either before or after the host plants (or simultaneously for a briefer but glorious display). Many can also be trained against house walls: a good way of growing plants that are not reliably hardy, since they will benefit from the reflected heat and extra shelter that the wall provides.

Above: Lonicera *has an intoxicating fragrance in the evening.*

Types of Climber

Climbing plants are usually categorized according to the way they cling (if they cling at all) to their support.

Twining climbers have stems that grow in a spiral, in the wild wrapping themselves around the stems of a host plant. The honeysuckles (*Lonicera*) are the most familiar example, but the group also includes the hop (*Humulus lupulus*) and wisteria. These plants are good for growing into trees or over trellis panels, either free-standing or attached to a wall.

Leaf stalk climbers, such as clematis, have specially adapted stalks that twist and grip the thin stems of a host plant. Some types of trellis are too coarse for these, so choose either a light trellis, pig wire or a framework of wires against a wall. They are also excellent rambling through shrubs.

Self-clinging climbers have special pads that adhere to the host, so no system of support is necessary. These are ideal for covering a wall.

Thorny plants, such as roses (*Rosa*), produce long, flexible stems that attach themselves to the bark of host plants by means of their sharp thorns. These usually need a little help in the garden. To train them into a tree, support the stems initially on long canes until the rose has a good grip. Against a wall, use a trellis or system of wires, and train the growing stems as near the horizontal as possible.

Above: 'Blairii No. 2', a sweetly scented
Bourbon rose, is repeat-flowering and can
make a spectacular climber.

Above: Free-flowering and prolific, this
particular Clematis montana *will scent
the air far and wide in late spring.*

A Scented Bower

For many, the scent of honeysuckle
defines summer, and it can be enjoyed
over a long period, since there are early-
and late-flowering forms. Equally familiar is the common jasmine (*Jasminum
officinale*). The sweet-scented *Jasminum
polyanthum* bears large clusters of
white flowers but is not hardy, so it
must be grown in a conservatory (sunroom) in cold areas. Even more richly
scented is the star jasmine (*Trachelospermum jasminoides*), an evergreen
with curious white flowers from
summer to autumn, that benefits from
the protection of a warm wall.

Another plant that benefits from the
support of a warm wall is wisteria,
surely the most dramatic of all flowering
climbers. In this case, the plant is fully
hardy, but it needs a good roasting in
summer to ensure that it flowers well
the following year. Wisteria is also

spectacular when it is grown
more informally, through a large
deciduous tree.

It is a pity that the large-flowered
clematis are mostly unscented. For
fragrance you need to look to the
smaller flowered species. *Clematis
montana* is a rampant plant, but not
all cultivars are scented. Curiously, a
montana can lose its scent from one
year to the next for no apparent
reason. The deliciously scented
Clematis flammula and *C. rehderiana*
are particularly valued for their late
season – from late summer to autumn.

SCENTED CLIMBERS

Akebia quinata
Clematis (some)
Jasminum
Lonicera (some)
Rosa
Trachelospermum jasminoides
Wisteria

GROUND-COVER PLANTS

There are a few useful, stalwart plants that can provide scent as well as fulfilling the overriding need to cover large areas of otherwise bare ground or to create weed-suppressing mats of herbage.

Violets make excellent ground cover, especially in a woodland garden, where they revel in the cool, slightly damp conditions. Another valuable woodlander is lily-of-the-valley (*Convallaria majalis*), provided you can get it established. It is also attractive in a shady rock garden. In a more open site (but still with some shelter), primulas could be charming, but remember that not all species are fragrant.

For covering large tracts of rough ground, *Crambe cordifolia* can be magnificent, although it must be admitted that not everyone finds the scent of the clouds of white summer

> SCENTED GROUND-
> COVER PLANTS
>
> *Cistus*
> *Convallaria majalis*
> *Crambe cordifolia*
> *Dianthus*
> *Geranium macrorrhizum*
> *Melissa*
> *Mentha*
> *Petasites*
> *Thymus*
> *Verbena*

flowers appealing. Another perennial, *Geranium macrorrhizum*, has velvety-textured leaves that emit a resinous fragrance when bruised. They have the added distinction of turning red in autumn.

Many climbers can be used as ground cover, particularly over a bank. Peg down the stems to encourage rooting. Besides strengthening the plant, this will keep down weeds.

Above: Applemint, like all the mints, makes good aromatic ground cover – perhaps too good, as it can be invasive.

Above: Houttuynia cordata *is a fine plant for ground cover or as a bog plant; the leaves smell of oranges when crushed.*

WATER PLANTS

Many water lilies are scented, but in a large pool it can be difficult to get close enough to appreciate this. You are more likely to catch the fragrance of plants at the water's edge.

The sweet rush (*Acorus calamus*) has deliciously scented, handsome, sword-like leaves and can be grown either in wet soil or in shallow water as a marginal plant. The straight species is of scant ornamental value, and only the variegated form, 'Variegatus', is widely grown.

An intriguing bog plant, which can also be grown in borders provided the soil does not dry out, is *Houttuynia cordata*, which has attractive arrow-shaped leaves that look as though cast in bronze. Crush a leaf between your fingers, however, and you will find it

*Above: Many water lilies (*Nymphaea*) are described as fragrant. But how are you supposed to get close enough to tell?*

smells distinctly of Seville (Temple) oranges. The cultivar 'Flore Pleno' has appealing double white flowers; 'Chameleon' has attractive leaves that are marbled with yellow and red. All forms make excellent ground cover.

All species of mint (*Mentha*) prefer reliably moist soil, but water mint (*M. aquatica*) actually likes to have its feet in water. A rather coarse plant, it can be invasive if given its head.

SCENTED BOG AND WATER PLANTS

Acorus calamus 'Variegatus'
Houttuynia cordata
Mentha aquatica
Nymphaea
Primula

31

PLANTS FOR CONTAINERS

All gardeners enjoy growing plants in containers. If you have only a patio garden, courtyard, balcony or roof space they are pretty much your only option, but even those who possess a large garden can see the benefits of containers. For one thing, they allow you to grow a wider range of plants than you could in the open garden. Use them for exotics of doubtful hardiness which can be moved inside in winter for enjoyment and protection.

Another advantage is that you can move the plants around the garden at will, bringing them into prominence on the patio when in full flower, moving them into the background at other times. Containers can form an important element of garden design. Large containers with identical plantings look very stylish arranged evenly

> SCENTED PLANTS FOR CONTAINERS
> *Alyssum maritimum*
> *Dianthus*
> *Heliotropium arborescens*
> *Hyacinthus orientalis*
> *Iris reticulata*
> *Lilium regale*
> *Muscari armeniacum*
> *Pelargonium* (scented-leaf)
> *Reseda odorata*
> *Rhododendron*
> *Skimmia japonica*

around a formal pool. For an integrated effect stick to matching containers, but in an informal garden an interesting mixture of styles can be charming.

Soil type places some restrictions on what you can grow in the garden, and containers allow you to overcome such problems. If you thought you could not grow rhododendrons because your soil is alkaline, think again. These plants thrive in containers, provided that you choose an ericaceous compost (acid soil mix).

The most suitable plants for containers are compact and preferably not too quick-growing. Dome-like shrubs, such as skimmias and the Mexican orange blossom (*Choisya ternata*), are ideal. Many conifers make a good choice, and a pair of upright junipers, such as *Juniperus* 'Blue Arrow', would look elegant.

On a smaller scale, carnations and pinks (*Dianthus*) appreciate the improved drainage of containers.

Above: A huge range of fragrant plants can be grown in containers.

The same goes for bulbs, and pots of hyacinths (*Hyacinthus*) and *Lilium regale* are almost essential in any garden worthy of the name.

Annuals thrive in containers, and this gives you the opportunity to experiment with colour combinations before you try them in the open garden. Be sure to add a few seeds of night-scented stock (*Matthiola longipetala* subsp. *bicornis*).

Baskets and Window Boxes

Most hanging baskets and window boxes are planned for their visual impact, but the power of scent need by no means be left out of the equation. A few scented-leaf plants, such as pelargoniums or prostrate rosemary, give an added dimension, and the scent will be readily released as you reach up or over to rub their leaves.

Above: Grow scented rhododendrons in containers of acid compost (soil mix). This is the sweetly scented 'Narcissiflorum'.

Sweet alyssum (*Lobularia maritima*) is a neat, tufty plant, ideal for the edge of a basket.

For a spring basket plant dwarf bulbs, such as grape hyacinths (*Muscari*) or narcissi. You need never be without scent in winter – look out for winter-flowering heathers (*Erica*) and pansies (*Viola*). Not all pansies are scented, so shop around for plants in bloom and be guided by your nose.

Above: Winter-flowering heathers make for a container with long-lasting appeal.

SCENTED PLANTS FOR
HANGING BASKETS
Dianthus
Jasminum polyanthum
Lavandula
Lobularia maritima
Muscari armeniacum
Narcissus
Pelargonium (scented-leaved)
Petunia (blue-flowered)
Primula
Rosmarinus
Viola

Caring for Container Plants

Plants in containers need rather more tender loving care than those grown in the open garden.

In cold areas, frost protection may be necessary in winter. Ideally, bring the plants under cover, such as into a conservatory (sunroom), greenhouse or porch. Sometimes the shelter of a carport can be adequate. If a pot is too heavy to move, wrap it in bubble wrap or an old blanket or sweater to protect the roots. A length of horticultural fleece (or even an old net curtain or sheets of newspaper) thrown over the plant will protect the top-growth.

In the growing season water your containers regularly: there is no residual moisture as there is in garden soil. At the height of summer you may need to water once or more every day so that the soil does not dry out. Ideally, water in the evening, when moisture will be slower to evaporate.

Feed plants when in growth, since the nutrients in potting compost (soil mix) are quickly exhausted. Pelleted fertilizers are the easiest to use. For permanent plantings, either replace the compost annually or, if this is not possible, scrape away the surface compost to a depth of at least 2.5cm (1in) and replace with fresh.

THE INDOOR GARDEN

Most house and conservatory plants are strictly foliage plants: either they do not flower in cultivation or the flowers are inconspicuous.

There are a few honourable exceptions, however. Bulbs, such as freesias and hyacinths (*Hyacinthus*), are usually

Above: Iris reticulata *can be grown in shallow pans of gritty compost. Discard forced bulbs after flowering, since they are unlikely to flower again.*

Above: Hyacinths – here with a primula – can be grown from specially prepared bulbs to supply mid-winter scent indoors.

Above: Narcissus papyraceus *is an excellent choice for growing in a container for an indoor display.*

intended for a temporary display and can be discarded after flowering. Rather longer lived are members of the genus *Citrus*, which are fragrant in all their parts, with oil-rich leaves and sweetly scented flowers and fruits. Once established, fruits will be virtually permanently present, since they take a year to ripen.

One of the most desirable of all conservatory plants is the gardenia, but it is temperamental, needing acid soil and a fairly even temperature – no draughts – in a lightly shaded place with a level of humidity most of us prefer to eliminate from the home. That said, the scent of the ivory-white flowers, produced from summer to autumn, is incomparable. Far easier

to cultivate are the many hybrid orchids that are now available. Many of the modern introductions have been bred to withstand the warm, dry air of the average centrally heated living room, and there are numerous winter- and spring-flowering cultivars. Look for plants in flower to be sure of getting a scented form.

SCENTED PLANTS FOR THE HOUSE
Citrus
Cyclamen persicum
Freesia
Gardenia augusta
Hyacinthus
Jasminum polyanthum
Narcissus papyraceus
Narcissus 'Soleil d'Or'
Orchids

Scent for All Seasons

IF YOU CHOOSE CAREFULLY FROM THE MANY SCENTED PLANTS AVAILABLE, YOU WILL BE ABLE TO ENJOY FRAGRANCE IN THE GARDEN THROUGHOUT THE YEAR. THE FOLLOWING PAGES DESCRIBE AND ILLUSTRATE A SELECTION OF PLANTS FOR EACH SEASON.

THE FRAGRANT GARDEN

A surprisingly large number of plants produce scent all year round. Conifers are always fragrant, though obviously you will be more aware of this during hot, dry weather in summer when the resin oozes from the branches. It is well worth passing your hands over the leaves in the dead of winter to remind yourself of their invigorating scent. All the woody evergreen herbs, such as bay (*Laurus nobilis*) and rosemary (*Rosmarinus*), retain their scent all year round, as do other evergreens, such as skimmias and choisyas.

Indoors, scented-leaf pelargoniums and citrus can be relied on to provide scent for all seasons.

Planning for Scent

Achieving year-round scent in your garden will be a matter of trial and error. Plant catalogues and encyclopedias are often vague when it comes to flowering times – necessarily so, since this can vary with the weather from year to year and will also depend on the local conditions.

For scent in winter, look to those shrubs that flower intermittently during mild periods, such as *Viburnum × bodnantense*, which has intensely fragrant, deep pink flowers from late autumn to spring. Spring flowers begin with dwarf bulbs, then come the magnolias and shrubs, many divinely scented. Summer is the peak of the

*Above: Aromatic bay (*Laurus nobilis*) is one of the most desirable of all evergreens.*

gardening year, when you can hardly count the different scents: this is the season of peonies, roses and all the many deliciously perfumed annuals.

Autumn is a quiet time in the garden, when everything in it is dying back – a season for taking stock of your successes and failures. This is a good time for planting to plug all those gaps in the succession of scent that you noticed throughout the year. But as you do so, you will also catch the scents of ripening fruits and seeds. And the deliciously sweet-scented ice plant (*Sedum spectabile*), beloved of bees, often flowers well into autumn.

Above: Fragrant in all their parts, the various members of the Citrus *genus provide year-round scent but need winter protection in cold areas.*

Above: A scented-leaf pelargonium will provide fragrance when you touch the plant, perhaps most noticeably in warm, dry weather.

SPRING

Many gardeners' favourite season, spring is the time when everything is fresh and full of promise. Most spring scents are appropriately fresh, light and airy.

Bulbs and Corms

Many spring bulbs produce scented flowers. Among the many daffodils and narcissi, those with short cups tend to have the sweetest fragrance, especially the Tazetta hybrids, such as 'Geranium' and 'Cragford'. *Iris reticulata* is delicious but unfortunately not reliably perennial. Dwarf bulbs that will multiply year after year include *Crocus tommasinianus* or forms of *C. chrysanthus*. Some of the more robust hybrids are

Above: *Viburnum carlesii 'Diana' has one of the richest fragrances of any of the spring-flowering shrubs.*

strong enough to compete with grass and can be planted to create scented drifts in a lawn. Prolific to the extent of becoming weeds are the sweetly scented grape hyacinths (*Muscari*).

Queen of all the spring bulbs, at least so far as scent goes, is the hyacinth (*Hyacinthus*). In appearance flowers are stiff and uncompromising: they are best grown in formal beds *en masse* if you have the space; otherwise they are ideal in containers.

Few tulips are scented – they have been bred for flamboyance of flower – but you could try the dainty lady tulip, *Tulipa clusiana*. To add scent to a dramatic bed of hybrid tulips, combine them with biennial wallflowers (*Cheiranthus*), which have perhaps the spiciest, most evocative perfume of any of the spring flowers. Look for dwarf varieties in shades that will complement the tulips.

Shrubs and Perennials

If you have acid soil, try some of the azaleas (*Rhododendron*). Not all cultivars are scented, but those that are often have a rich, lily-like fragrance entirely in keeping with their exotic-looking flowers.

Spring is the season of viburnums, such as *V. × burkwoodii* and *V. carlesii*, both richly perfumed and tolerant of any soil. There is rich scent to be found among the skimmias, which have a powerful lily-of-the-valley fragrance.

Skimmias are extremely versatile and make an elegant choice for containers and tubs near the front door with their squat, compact habit.

If you have light, acid soil, the tree heath (*Erica arborea*) will be a joy in this season with its honey-scented flowers. More tolerant of a range of soil types are the berberises and the handsome *Osmanthus decorus*.

Among perennials, do not overlook lily-of-the-valley (*Convallaria majalis*), a modest plant that is charming where allowed to push itself up through cracks in paving. It is one of the few scented plants that thrives in shade.

Above: *The herbaceous* Clematis recta *is scented, unlike the large-flowered climbing hybrids.*

Climbers and Trees

There are not many climbers that flower in spring, and those that do tend to have no scent. However, two clematis are worth having for their scent. The evergreen *C. armandii* is handsome, with vanilla-scented flowers around

mid-spring. More rampant is *C. montana*. Cultivars vary, but 'Elizabeth' (pale pink) and 'Alexander' (white) are sweetly scented.

Ornamental cherries and magnolias are generally chosen for their looks rather than their scent, but many will reliably perfume the air as well. Among magnolias, *M. denudata* is ravishing, with large flowers that open before the leaves unfurl. *M. salicifolia* has orange-blossom-scented flowers.

For later in the season, consider some of the crab apples (*Malus*), with their delicate blossoms, and lilacs (*Syringa*), which take the shrub season into summer with what is perhaps the most wonderfully potent scent in the entire garden.

SCENTED PLANTS FOR SPRING

Clematis armandii
Convallaria majalis
Crocus
Erica arborea
Erysimum cheiri
Hyacinthus
Magnolia (some)
Muscari armeniacum
Narcissus (some)
Primula (some)
Rhododendron (some)
Syringa
Viburnum

39

SUMMER

This is the peak of the gardening year, when the well-planned garden will be filled with an apparently unending succession of flowers. At this time of year, there is an abundance of choice to ensure that delicious scents greet you whenever you step outside on a sunny morning.

Shrubs and Perennials

The summer season is heralded by the peonies, stately plants with gorgeous flowers that are usually of an intoxicating spiciness matched by no other group of plants. Old-fashioned forms of clove-scented carnations and pinks (*Dianthus*) also have a part to play, provided you can supply the conditions that suit them – well-drained, alkaline soil in full sun. Some do best in a rock garden.

Summer is the season of roses, and no garden worthy of the name should be without them. All rose scents are appealing, but while some are light and fresh, others have deeper base notes that make them richer and more complex. One of the best is the climber 'New Dawn', which has a very pronounced, but not cloying, fruity scent that is at its best towards the end of the season as the nights become cooler and damper.

A group of roses known as hybrid musks includes the delightful 'Buff Beauty', with deliciously fragrant flowers of soft apricot-orange that

Above: Like all of the mock oranges, the cultivar Philadelphus *'Belle Etoile' possesses a rich scent.*

Above: If you have acid soil, plant the heather Erica vagans *'Summertime', which prefers such conditions.*

fades to a creamy white in sun. The rambling rose 'Albertine' is virtually unsurpassed for scent, although the myrrh-like notes of 'Constance Spry' run it close. Among modern roses, the aptly named 'Fragrant Cloud' has a rich scent that hangs on the air. 'Margaret Merril' is also incomparable for a white garden. The bleached mauve of 'Blue Moon' does not appeal to all tastes, but the scent is full and lemony.

Mock oranges (*Philadelphus*) are richly, even cloyingly scented. The flowers are exclusively white. 'Virginal' is a good double, but eventually makes a large shrub up to 3m (10ft) in both directions. The cultivar 'Belle Etoile' has single flowers with appeal-ing purple blotches at the centre.

Above: Genista lydia, *which flowers in early summer, is a fine scented plant for a Mediterranean-style garden.*

P. coronarius 'Aureus' has the added distinction of yellow-green leaves, but needs a sheltered position out of full sun to avoid scorching.

SCENTED PLANTS FOR SUMMER
Buddleja
Cestrum parqui
Clematis recta
Clematis rehderiana
Hesperis matronalis
Lilium regale
Lonicera (some)
Matthiola longipetala subsp. *bicornis*
Nicotiana
Philadelphus
Syringa
Wisteria

Trees

Scented summer-flowering trees are rare but delicious. In the past, limes (*Tilia*) were a popular choice for avenues leading up to stately homes, and now they are mature we can enjoy their fragrance. The pale yellow flowers, though they look insignificant, have an unforgettable scent.

In a small garden, the Mount Etna broom (*Genista aetnensis*) is a good choice. It is a light, airy tree that casts little shade but pours forth its fragrant yellow flowers at the height of summer. It needs a well-drained spot in full sun. Sophoras are equally desirable, but not all the species are hardy, and even those that are need long, hot summers to flower reliably.

Annuals and Biennials

Mignonette (*Reseda odorata*) is a charmingly old-fashioned flower with a sweet scent, ideal for a cottage garden. Stocks (*Matthiola*) are also fragrant, and there are many strains of varying colours. The spires of gillyflowers (*M. incana*) are in white and shades of pink, mauve, violet and purple. Sweet alyssum (*Lobularia maritima*), in white or purple, is low-growing and makes an excellent edging plant. Where happy, it will seed itself obligingly in paving cracks. Look out for new strains of another cottage garden favourite, sweet William (*Dianthus barbatus*), which will flower the same year as it is sown and make an invaluable addition to the border.

Above: Buddleja davidii 'Peace' is a white form of this highly fragrant species.

Night-scented Flowers

For flowers that are fragrant in the evening look to the aptly named night-scented stock (*Matthiola longipetala* subsp. *bicornis*) or to tobacco plants (*Nicotiana*). These hang their heads in the most pensive way during the heat of the day but revive as the temperature falls to release a potent, incense-like fragrance. *Hesperis matronalis* has the charming common names of dame's violet or sweet rocket. The flowers, which are mauve, purple or white, are carried in phlox-like heads.

Cestrum parqui, a sub-shrub of borderline hardiness, possesses panicles of curious, star-like, lime green flowers. You realize the point of the plant as night falls, when the flowers release a unique, bubble-gum fragrance to attract the night-flying moths that

Above: Paeonia '*Alice Harding*', like nearly all the hybrid peonies, has spicily scented flowers.

pollinate them. Position the plant in a warm corner of the garden where you relax in the evening.

Herbs

Most of the aromatic herbs are at their best in summer, when their essential oils are freely produced. On a really hot day, the curry plant (*Helichrysum italicum*) will give off its characteristic spicy odour without you having to bruise its leaves. The sweetly scented flowers of lavender (*Lavandula*) and thyme (*Thymus*) are a must, both for their unforgettable fragrance and their attraction for bees and other insects. Lavender can also be harvested and dried for scenting lines.

AUTUMN

Scents tend to be in short supply at this time of year, when most plants are busy setting seed and ripening their fruits. Many of the autumn-flowering plants have no scent at all, though it is worth keeping an eye on new dahlia hybrids: scented forms are being developed using a species that has not hitherto made its way into the garden.

Cheating Nature

Until such time as scented dahlias are widely available, we have to rely on a few tricks. For scent in the autumn garden, you can make a few late sowings of fragrant annuals to be planted out from midsummer. Tobacco plants (*Nicotiana*) will carry on flowering until the first frosts and will reward you with their deliciously scented flowers well into autumn. Pruning *Buddleja davidii* in late spring will delay its flowering season, and as long as the summer is not too hot, flowers should still be coming at this time of year.

Many roses have an autumn display that matches the summer one. 'Buff Beauty' is, if anything, even better in autumn, since the flowers hold their distinctive soft orange colour for longer before they fade to white.

In a good year, you can expect the evergreen *Magnolia grandiflora* to push out a few more flowers in autumn. In a cold area train this against a warm wall or look for the cultivar 'Victoria', which is apparently

Above: *Plants from a late sowing of white* Nicotiana, *here planted with white* Heliotropium, *will continue to flower well into the autumn.*

Above: Most crab apples not only bear fragrant spring flowers but also have aromatic fruits.

*Above: The medlar (*Mespilus germanica*) has edible fruits that develop a honeyed sweetness when softened by frost.*

impervious to the cold. There is no need to cheat nature in the case of *Elaeagnus* × *ebbingei*, as it actually flowers at this time of year. All its cultivars are evergreen and some are attractively variegated. The flowers are inconspicuous but exude a sweet, powerful scent even on chilly days.

Fruits and Foliage

Apples and pears are well known, but the queen of fruits so far as scent is concerned must be the quince (*Cydonia oblonga*). Pick a few and place them in a bowl in a warm room, where they will soon release their distinctive sweet and spicy aroma. They are not edible raw, but make a sublime addition to apple pies and crumbles. Quince jelly is a precious treat. The fruits of the little-grown

medlar (*Mespilus germanica*) develop their fragrance as they begin to rot after the first frost; indeed, this is the point at which they become edible.

The leaves of walnuts (*Juglans*) and *Cercidiphyllum japonicum* are also unusually fragrant after they have fallen from the tree, bringing a special pleasure to an autumn stroll through any woodland or arboretum where they are planted.

> ### SCENTED PLANTS FOR AUTUMN
> *Acidanthera bicolor*
> *Amaryllis belladonna*
> *Camellia sasanqua*
> *Cercidiphyllum japonicum*
> *Chaenomeles*
> *Cydonia oblonga*
> *Elaeagnus* × *ebbingei*
> *Juglans*
> *Magnolia grandiflora*
> *Mespilus germanica*

WINTER

Far from being a dead time of year, winter is a season when the garden can be full of scent. Indeed, the fragrance of a winter garden seems to have an added poignancy when so much is lifeless and barren.

Winter Shrubs

One of the best shrubs is the witch hazel (*Hamamelis mollis*) which has spidery, ochre yellow flowers that are sweetly scented. It will do best in a sheltered spot and prefers acid to neutral soil. It is slow-growing, so it will be some years before you will feel happy about cutting branches for indoors. Another desirable plant is the

Above: The winter flowers of sarcococca have an almost overpowering scent and are quite happy to grow in shade.

winter-sweet, *Chimonanthus praecox*, although this, too, is slow-growing. Rather faster are the excellent sarcococcas, low-growing evergreens with glossy, pointed leaves. They make excellent ground cover, even under trees. The scent of the inconspicuous white flowers is almost overpowering, and even a couple of branches brought into the warm indoors will scent the whole house.

Viburnum × *bodnantense* is excellent and reliable, flowering on and off throughout winter. Of even greater distinction is *Daphne bholua*, which benefits from a sheltered spot. Plant it near the front door so that you can appreciate its incomparable scent.

A number of shrubs are of small value when in leaf but earn their keep through the fragrance of their winter

Above: Viburnum × bodnantense *'Dawn' is one of the most sweetly-scented of all winter-flowering shrubs.*

Above: Daphne bholua *is a wonderful shrub for planting near the front door, where visitors will appreciate its scent.*

flowers. One such is the shrubby honeysuckle, *Lonicera fragrantissima*, a good plant for a wild garden.

On a warm wall, you could try *Acacia dealbata*, which produces fluffy yellow flowers towards the end of winter. In mild areas this makes an excellent specimen tree. Another plant that benefits from wall protection is *Abeliophyllum distichum*, with fragrant, white, forsythia-like flowers.

SCENTED PLANTS FOR WINTER

Abeliophyllum distichum
Acacia dealbata
Chimonanthus praecox
Daphne bholua
Hamamelis mollis
Iris unguicularis
Lonicera fragrantissima
Mahonia × media
Sarcococca
Viburnum × bodnantense

A Special Iris

The Algerian iris (*Iris unguicularis*) is unique. It produces its large flowers in the depths of winter. To appreciate them to the full, pull them from the plant while they are still in bud and watch them unfurl in a warm sitting-room, where they will release a delicious fragrance. The plant itself is tough and hardy, but, betraying its geographical origins, it needs a hot position (preferably at the base of a warm wall) in well-drained soil of low fertility. Once established, it should be left alone, and the flowering display will improve year on year, as long as the rhizome gets a good baking in the previous summer.

Above: The yellow flowers of Mahonia × media *bring the fragrance of lily-of-the-valley to the winter garden.*

47

Scent for Every Style

TELEVISION MAKEOVER PROGRAMMES AND STYLE MAGAZINES HAVE MADE DESIGNERS OF ALL OF US, AND NOW NEARLY ALL GARDENERS CONSIDER DESIGN AN ESSENTIAL ASPECT IF THE GARDEN IS TO BE MORE THAN JUST A COLLECTION OF PLANTS.

DEFINING STYLE

In gardening the word style is a convenient way of categorizing or of sorting plants into groups and arrangements that seem homogeneous, meaningful and aesthetically pleasing. When we design a garden or a section of a garden, we will choose plants that will help us create the effects we want to achieve, opting, for example, for those with a regular shape, such as many conifers or skimmias, or those that can be clipped and topiarized, such as box or privet, to create a formal garden. A cottage garden style implies a more relaxed approach to both planting and weed control, involving plants that are easy to cultivate and do not need endless trimming and pruning to look their best. If, in addition to achieving a particular visual style, we want to incorporate scented plants,

Above: Aromatic herb gardens can be defined by formal, clipped hedges.

Above: Terracotta containers are perfect
for growing informal groupings of
aromatic herbs.

Above: Camomile can be used to create a
fragrant lawn that needs no mowing and
releases scent as you walk over it.

our plans might need to be modified
to varying degrees to accommodate
this extra dimension.

SELECTING A STYLE

The overall guideline that you should
select a style for your garden that
reflects your own personality and
lifestyle is a truism, but it is nevertheless worth observing: there is no point
opting for a garden that relies on
summer bedding for scent, colour and
definition if you do not have time to
raise, plant out and then lift the spent
plants at the end of the season. Given
this caveat, however, there is a wide
range of styles that can be adapted
to include the many scented plants
described in the previous section.

When scent is as important a factor
in your garden design as colour or
ease of maintenance, your plant selection should reflect this. It is well
known that some roses, for example,
are more fragrant than others, and
this is true of several other plant
groups. There are many more cultivars and strains available today than
in the past, but even given this vast
choice, there may be occasions when
your wish to include a fragrant plant
may have to override other design
considerations, such as colour or
form. Nevertheless, the gardener who
longs for scent will find plants of
almost every conceivable shape,
colour and habit of growth to fit in
with the most demanding of schemes.

COTTAGE GARDEN

The idealized picture of a cottage garden, with bees buzzing lazily above lavender and other sweetly scented flowers, is an appealing one, even if it exists more in the popular imagination than in reality. Contrary to what you might expect, planting a scented cottage garden requires the ruthless selection of fragrant cultivars and the exclusion of other, strongly growing but less aromatic varieties.

Choosing Plants

Typically, the cottage garden consists of simple plants that are easy to grow. The beds and borders should be over-flowing with a profusion of plants.

Borders can be edged with box or lavender, both fragrant in different ways, which may be formally clipped or allowed to grow more freely. Roses

Above: Skimmia japonica *is a useful evergreen shrub with sweetly scented flowers in early spring.*

are essential, but choose from the many scented varieties. Old roses are traditional, but many flower only once, and there is no reason to exclude modern roses that have a longer season.

For climbers, think about the climbing roses ('Zéphirine Drouhin' is an old favourite, with magenta flowers over a long period), jasmine or honey-suckles. If these can be persuaded to frame the front door or sitting room window, so much the better. If you have a garden gate, it is a charming idea to train climbing plants over an archway spanning the path at the entrance to the garden.

Perennials include scented pinks (*Dianthus*); some have appealing names, such as 'Gran's Favourite', 'Sops in Wine' and 'Fair Folly'. Peonies, such as hybrids of *Paeonia officinalis* (often sold unnamed), are cottage garden

Above: Scented roses in profusion are an essential part of cottage garden style.

Above: A cottage garden is a pleasing jumble of colourful and fragrant plants, at its best in high summer.

classics. All the perennial herbs belong in such a garden; traditionally they were used to provide potpourri and were often spread on the floor to cover damp smells, to say nothing of their value in the kitchen and as medicines. The Madonna lily (*Lilium candidum*), with white, scented flowers, is also a typical cottage garden plant. For annuals, try dame's violet (*Hesperis matronalis*), old-fashioned tobacco plants (*Nicotiana*) and sweet peas (*Lathyrus odoratus*), which can also be incorporated in a vegetable plot to provide cut flowers for the house.

*Above: Fragrant cottage garden pinks (*Dianthus*) have been grown for centuries.*

SCENTED COTTAGE GARDEN PLANTS
Convallaria majalis
Dianthus
Geranium macrorrhizum
Hesperis matronalis
Lathyrus odoratus
Lilium
Lobularia maritima
Matthiola
Nicotiana
Paeonia officinalis
Philadelphus
Reseda odorata
Rosa

51

MEDITERRANEAN GARDEN

In recent years, as climate change has made summers in much of the northern hemisphere drier and hotter, the Mediterranean-style garden has become increasingly popular. This popularity has been fuelled by an increased use of aromatic herbs in the kitchen and by the fact that many of these herbs are not only attractive but also easy to maintain.

The Best Conditions

The Mediterranean style implies a warm, sunny site and soil that is both free-draining and low in fertility. Lushness is the antithesis of this style. Basking in heat and starved of nutrients, Mediterranean plants develop a gaunt appearance that is an essential part of their appeal.

A sun-baked slope is ideal. Most Mediterranean plants do not mind wind, and some are coastal. White concrete terraces will help to reflect heat and light, as will a top-dressing of gravel, which will also improve drainage – vital for all these plants.

Choosing Plants

Height and structure should really be provided by pines, which exude their resinous sap as the temperature climbs in summer. There are plenty of dwarf varieties for the small garden. That also goes for junipers (*Juniperus*), though these are a little less "giving" of their fragrance. Another traditional conifer of the Mediterranean is the cypress (*Cupressus sempervirens*). Elegant, pencil-thin forms are the most desirable. For a cold climate, be

Above: Using gravel allows you to grow a wide range of scented sun-loving plants.

Above: Citrus trees in pots are an essential feature of the Mediterranean garden.

Above: The distinctive scent of lavender is associated with the Mediterranean style.

sure to look out for the hardy forms that have been developed in recent years. Another excellent tree for this style of garden is the Mount Etna broom (*Genista aetnensis*) which produces a shower of yellow, scented pea blossom in summer but is so light and airy that it casts little shade.

Bulk out the borders with the excellent cistuses, grown mainly for their crinkled, papery summer flowers but of value here for their sticky, resinous stems and leaves. All the woody herbs suit this style of gardening.

Many favourite culinary herbs are indispensable additions to this type of garden and can be used to provide colour as well as scent. Lavender and rosemary are obvious candidates. Remember box (*Buxus sempervirens*), an excellent edging plant that can be clipped to shape or not, as the fancy

takes you. Box borders have been discovered in excavations of Roman villas, so there is classical precedence for its use. It has a quite distinctive scent that is released during hot weather or after a shower and that most gardeners learn to love.

SCENTED PLANTS FOR A
MEDITERRANEAN GARDEN

Artemisia
Buxus sempervirens
Cistus
Citrus
Cupressus sempervirens
Genista aetnensis
Helichrysum italicum
Juniperus
Laurus nobilis
Lavandula stoechas
Olea europea
Phlomis fruticosa
Pinus
Rosmarinus
Salvia officinalis

FORMAL GARDEN

The formal style is more a matter of design than the other garden types discussed in this book. The gardener who is attracted to formalism is more interested in the structure and shape of the garden – what might be referred to as the manipulation of an exterior space – than such incidentals as flowers. Nevertheless, scent need not be excluded from such a scheme.

Choosing Plants

While formality can be achieved through non-plant material, through the lie of paths, walls and formal pools, it would be almost a contradiction in terms to banish plants from the

Above: *Use scented bedding plants as a backdrop to formal features.*

garden entirely. Plants that lend themselves to clipping obviously answer well the requirements of formalism. Unfortunately, extensive pruning – a gardening discipline in its own right – is often carried out at the expense of flowers. This is where plants with scented leaves come into their own. Box (*Buxus sempervirens*) is ideal for edging a planting area, in containers or clipped to shape.

Less versatile, but with an equally distinctive smell, are the curry plant (*Helichrysum italicum*) and lavender (*Lavandula*). A few tastefully positioned conifers, especially those that grow into a perfect shape without the intervention of the gardener, could complete a planting that would be low-key and subtle but would have the benefit of fragrance.

A specimen tree (possibly in a container) would make an excellent focal point. Bay (*Laurus nobilis*), with aromatic evergreen leaves, can be clipped to shape, though in some areas it needs some protection from cold, drying winds in winter (horticultural fleece would be adequate on a frosty night). An acacia (*Acacia dealbata*), citrus or olive (*Olea europea*), all with fragrant flowers, could also look extremely stylish, although none is reliably hardy.

If you cannot imagine life without flowers, consider the sculptural perfection of lilies. These can be grown in

Above: In a formal garden, a raised bed is an ideal way to bring scent as close as possible to the gardener.

SCENTED PLANTS FOR
A FORMAL GARDEN

Buxus sempervirens
Citrus
Conifers
Laurus nobilis
Lavandula
Ligustrum lucidum
Myrtus communis
Rosmarinus
Santolina

pots and distributed around the garden in a formal arrangement. Earlier in the year, hyacinths planted in containers would have a comparable distinction, and their stiff, upright habit is entirely apposite in these surroundings. Annuals recommended for bedding are excellent when they are grown in formal blocks. Look for single colour strains of stocks (*Matthiola*), tobacco plants (*Nicotiana*) – 'Lime Green' is a sophisticated choice – and sweet alyssum (*Lobularia maritima*).

Above: This formal garden has been filled with a range of plants to appeal to the senses, including roses and lavender.

MODERN GARDEN

The essence of the modern style is determined by a desire for simplicity. A contemporary garden is based on pure form and texture, creating an environment that is both stimulating and calming. The planting must be carefully considered and should consist of a focused palette of scented plants, are promoted. The beautifully scented *Lilium* 'Star Gazer' is an example of a bulb that is currently in vogue. Its deep, rose-red flowers, edged with white, is perfect for adding a splash of colour to a muted, contemporary scene. Other scented lilies that are suitable for a modern setting are *Lilium regale* with its large, trumpet-shaped white flowers and *Lilium candidum*, the Madonna lily.

Choosing Plants

No plant is actually modern in the generally accepted sense of the term, but trends in gardening come and go. Plants fall in and out of favour, partly as a result of television pro-grammes and partly as new cultivars

Hostas can be grand and architec-tural, but they are usually grown for their leaves rather than their flowers. The exceptions are *H. plantaginea* and a hybrid derived from it, 'Honeybells'. Both of these have shining green

Above: *This sleek, black slate bench, with lilies planted close by, provides the perfect resting place to sit and enjoy the fragrances of the garden.*

*Above: Cotton lavender (*Santolina) *grows in a pleasing dome shape that lends itself to contemporary plantings.*

Genetic modification will no doubt be used to introduce scent into previously unscented flowers, such as gladioli and chrysanthemums, but in the meantime, the modern gardener looks to such plants as *Yucca filamentosa*, a perennial with spiky, sword-like leaves and panicles of scented white flowers in late summer, *Mahonia × media*, a group of gaunt shrubs with richly fragrant, yellow flowers in winter above pointed, holly-like leaves, or the stiffly formal hyacinths (*Hyacinthus*), which flower in spring. All have the characteristic high-tech look that is appropriate to a garden designed in a contemporary style.

leaves and sweetly scented white flowers in the summer, and unlike most hostas, they are best in full sun. Both are excellent in containers.

One of the most architectural of all herbaceous perennials is *Angelica archangelica* (sometimes a biennial), which carries its large, dome-shaped heads of greenish-yellow summer flowers on stems up to 2m (6ft) tall. It is aromatic in all its parts.

A High-tech Garden

The modern garden uses a range of materials. Galvanized, beaten metal containers are part of the style, as is recycled glass, often moulded into "pebbles" in place of gravel (which is less acceptable these days, since it is not a renewable resource). Even old CDs can be recycled for use as a paving material. The traditional colours of stone and terracotta are less in keeping with the high-tech style.

Above: A bank of highly scented hyacinths add colour and form.

Plants for Scent

MOST OF THE PLANTS LISTED BELOW ARE MORE FULLY DESCRIBED
ELSEWHERE IN THE BOOK, BUT THIS CHECKLIST IS PROVIDED AS A
QUICK REFERENCE TO HELP YOU CHOOSE A RANGE OF SCENTED
PLANTS FOR ALL SEASONS WHEN PLANNING YOUR GARDEN.

Plant name	Part of plant scented	Season	Day/night
Acacia t HH–FRH	flowers	winter–spring	day
Akebia quinata c FH	flowers	spring	day
Aloysia triphylla h FRH	leaves	spring–summer–autumn	day
Artemisia arborescens h FH	leaves	spring–summer–autumn	day
Berberis sargentiana h FH	flowers	spring	day
Buddleja s FH	flowers	summer–autumn	day
Camellia sasanqua s FH	flowers	autumn–winter	day
Cercidiphyllum t FH	fallen leaves	autumn	day
Cestrum parqui s FRH	flowers	summer–autumn	night
Choisya ternata s FH	flowers/leaves	spring	day
Cistus s FH	stems	summer	day
Citrus s/t FRH	flowers/leaves	all year	day
Clematis armandii c FH	flowers	spring	day
Clematis flammula c FH	flowers	summer–autumn	day
Clematis montana c FH	flowers	spring	day
Clematis recta p FH	flowers	spring–summer	day
Clematis rehderiana c FH	flowers	summer–autumn	day
Convallaria majalis p FH	flowers	spring	day
Cosmos atrosanguineus p FRH	flowers	summer	day
Crambe cordifolia p FH	flowers	summer	day
Crocus b FH	flowers	spring	day

Above: Crambe cordifolia

Above: Paeonia 'Bowl of Beauty'

Cytisus battandieri s FRH	flowers	summer	day
Daphne s FH–FRH	flowers	winter/spring	day
Deutzia s FH	flowers	spring–summer	day
Dianthus p/a FH	flowers	spring–summer	day
Elaeagnus × *ebbingei* s FH	flowers	autumn	day
Erica s FH–FRH	flowers	all seasons	day
Erysimum cheiri p FH	flowers	spring	day
Eucalyptus t FH	stems	all year	day
Genista aetnensis s/t FH	flowers	summer	day
Genista lydia s FH	flowers	summer	day
Hamamelis mollis s FH	flowers	winter	day
Hebe cupressoides s FH	stems	all year	day
Helichrysum italicum h FH	leaves	all year	day
Heliotropium arborescens a FH	flowers	summer	day
Hemerocallis p FH	flowers	summer	day/night
Hesperis matronalis bi FH	flowers	spring–summer	night
Hosta 'Honeybells' p FH	flowers	summer	day
Hosta plantaginea p FH	flowers	summer	day
Hyacinthus orientalis b FH	flowers	winter–spring	day
Hypericum 'Hidcote' s FH	leaves	spring–summer	day
Iris p/b FH	flowers/bulb	winter/spring/ summer	day
Jasminum c FH–FRH	flowers	winter/summer	day
Laurus nobilis s/h FRH	leaves	all year	day
Lavandula h FH–HH	flowers/leaves	spring/summer– autumn	day
Lilium b FH–HH	flowers	summer	day/night
Liquidambar styraciflua t FH	leaves	spring–summer	day
Lobularia maritima a FH	flowers	summer–autumn	day
Lonicera c/s FH	flowers	summer/winter	day
Magnolia s/t FH	flowers	spring	day
Mahonia s FH	flowers	winter–spring	day
Matthiola a FH	flowers	summer	day/night

Above: Dianthus *'Louise's Choice'*

Above: Lonicera japonica *'Halliana'*

Plants for Scent

Melissa h FH	leaves	spring–summer–autumn	day
Mentha h FH	leaves	spring–summer–autumn	day
Muscari b FH	flowers	spring	day
Myrtus s FRH	flowers	summer	day
Narcissus b FH–HH	flowers	spring	day
Nicotiana a FRH–HH	flowers	summer–autumn	night
Nymphaea wp FH–FRH	flowers	summer	day
Osmanthus s FH	flowers	spring	day
Paeonia s/p FH	flowers	spring–summer	day
Pelargonium p FRH (scented-leaf)	leaves	all year	day
Perovskia s FH	stems	spring–summer–autumn	day
Petasites p FH	flowers	winter–spring	day
Petunia a HH	flowers	summer	day
Philadelphus s FH	flowers	summer	day/ evening
Phlomis s FH–FRH	flowers	summer	day
Phlox p/al FH–HH	flowers	summer	day
Populus balsamifera t FH	leaves	spring	day
Primula p/al FH–FT	flowers	spring/summer	day
Reseda odorata a FH	flowers	spring–summer–autumn	day
Rhododendron s FH–FT	flowers	spring–summer	day
Rosa s/c FH	flowers	summer–autumn	day
Rosmarinus h FH–HH	leaves	all year	day
Ruta graveolens h FH	leaves	all year	day
Salix triandra s FH	flowers	winter–spring	day
Santolina s FH	leaves	all year	day
Sarcococca s FH	flowers	winter	day

Above: Pelargonium *'Little Gem'*

Above: Santolina chamaecyparissus

Skimmia s FH	flowers/leaves	winter–spring	day
Smilacina racemosa p FH	flowers	spring	day
Spartium junceum s FH	flowers	summer	day
Syringa s FH	flowers	spring	day
Thymus h FH	leaves	spring–summer	day
Trachelospermum c FRH *jasminoides*	flowers	summer	evening
Tulipa b FH	flowers	spring	day
Verbena p/a FH–FT	flowers	summer	day
Viburnum carlesii s FH	flowers	spring	day
Viburnum s FH × *bodnantense*	flowers	winter	day
Viola p/a FH	flowers	summer/winter	day
Wisteria c FH	flowers	summer	day

KEY TO ABBREVIATIONS

a = annual	c = climber	t = tree
al = alpine	h = herb	wp = water plant
b = bulb	p = perennial	
bi = biennial	s = shrub	

FT = frost tender = may be damaged by temperatures below 5°C (41°F)
HH = half hardy = can withstand temperatures down to 0°C (32°F)
FRH = frost hardy = can withstand temperatures down to –5°C (23°F)
FH = fully hardy = can withstand temperatures down to –15°C (5°F)

In the United States, throughout the Sun Belt states, from Florida, across the Gulf Coast, south Texas, southern deserts to Southern California and coastal regions, annuals are planted in the autumn, bloom in the winter and spring, and die at the beginning of summer.

Above: Rosa 'Ispahan'

Above: Ruta graveolens 'Variegata'

Common Names of Plants

THE FOLLOWING IS A LIST OF THE COMMON NAMES OF THE PLANTS
MENTIONED IN THIS BOOK. PLANTS WHOSE COMMON NAMES ARE
THE SAME AS THE BOTANIC NAME, SUCH AS CAMELLIAS AND HOSTAS,
ARE NOT INCLUDED HERE.

Balsam poplar
  Populus balsamifera
Barberry *Berberis sargentiana*
Basil *Ocimum basilicum*
Bay *Laurus nobilis*
Bergamot *Monarda*
Broom *Genista lydia*
Butterfly bush *Buddleja*
Carnation *Dianthus*
Cherry *Prunus*
Christmas box *Sarcococca*
Cotton lavender *Santolina*
Crab apple *Malus*
Curry plant
  Helichrysum italicum
Daffodil *Narcissus*
Dame's violet
  Hesperis matronalis
Daylily *Hemerocallis*
Grape hyacinth
  Muscari armeniacum
Gum *Eucalyptus*
Hawthorn *Crateagus*
Heather *Erica*
Heliotrope
  Heliotropium arborescens
Honeysuckle *Lonicera*
Hop *Humulus lupulus*
Hyacinth
  Hyacinthus orientalis
Jasmine *Jasminum*
Katsura tree *Cercidiphyllum*
Lavender *Lavandula*
Lemon balm *Melissa*
Lilac *Syringa*
Lily *Lilium*

Lily-of-the-valley
  Convallaria majalis
Lime tree *Tilia*
Medlar *Mespilus germanica*

Above: Narcissus *'Actaea'*.

Mexican orange blossom
  Choisya ternata
Mignonette *Reseda odorata*
Mint *Mentha*
Mock orange *Philadelphus*
Mount Etna broom
  Genista aetnensis
Myrtle *Myrtus*
Nasturtium *Tropaeolum*
Night-scented stock
  Matthiola longipetala
  subsp. *bicornis*
Oregon grape *Mahonia*
Pansy *Viola*
Pennyroyal *Mentha pulegium*
Peony *Paeonia*

Pineapple broom
  Cytisus battandieri
Pink *Dianthus*
Primrose *Primula*
Quince *Cydonia oblonga*
Rose *Rosa*
Rosemary *Rosmarinus*
Rue *Ruta graveolens*
Russian sage *Perovskia*
St John's wort *Hypericum*
  'Hidcote'
Star jasmine
  Trachelospermum
  jasminoides
Stock *Matthiola*
Sweet alyssum
  Lobularia maritima
Sweet briar *Rosa eglanteria*
Sweet pea *Lathyrus odoratus*
Sweet rocket
  Hesperis matronalis
Sweet William
  Dianthus barbatus
Sweet rush *Acorus calamus*
Thyme *Thymus*
Tobacco plant *Nicotiana*
Tulip *Tulipa*
Violet *Viola*
Virgin's bower
  Clematis flammula
Wallflower *Erysimum cheiri*
Wattle *Acacia*
Willow-leaved jessamine
  Cestrum parqui
Winter-sweet *Chimonanthus*
Witch hazel *Hamamelis mollis*

Index

***Above:** Aromatic pines are typically Mediterranean.*

Index

Above: *Sweet-scented*
Erysimum *'Bowles'*
Mauve' is a stalwart
of the spring garden.